SUBWAY CERAMICS

Subway Ceramics

A HISTORY AND ICONOGRAPHY

*of mosaic and bas relief signs and plaques
in the New York City subway system
with photographs by the author*

SECOND EDITION

Lee Stookey

LEE STOOKEY
BRATTLEBORO, VERMONT

for Byron

Subway Ceramics: A History and Iconography
Second Edition: October 1994

Text and illustrations copyright © 1992 and 1994 by Lee Stookey

All photographs taken by the author, with permission of
the New York City Transit Authority, between 1972 and 1974
(except pages 29, 35, 39, 43, 45, 53 and 87 taken in 1994)

Map designed by John Tauranac. Copyright © 1992 by Tauranac, Ltd. All rights reserved.

Dates of station openings from the *Bulletin* of
the Electric Railroaders Association, New York Division

Designed by Barbara DuPree Knowles
Produced by BDK Books, Inc., New York, New York

Printed in the United States of America by
The William J. Mack Co., North Haven, Connecticut

Library of Congress Catalog Card Number: 94-66996
ISBN 0-9635486-1-1

Published by Lee Stookey
9 NORTH STREET, BRATTLEBORO, VERMONT 05301   (800) 257-4694
To order, send $15 plus $1.75 for mailing.

CONTENTS

A NOTE ABOUT THE SECOND EDITION: Seven new photographs,
taken in 1994, replace ones used in the first edition; and minor corrections
and changes have been made in the text.

ILLUSTRATIONS

NOTE: The map on the facing page shows only the above listed stations.

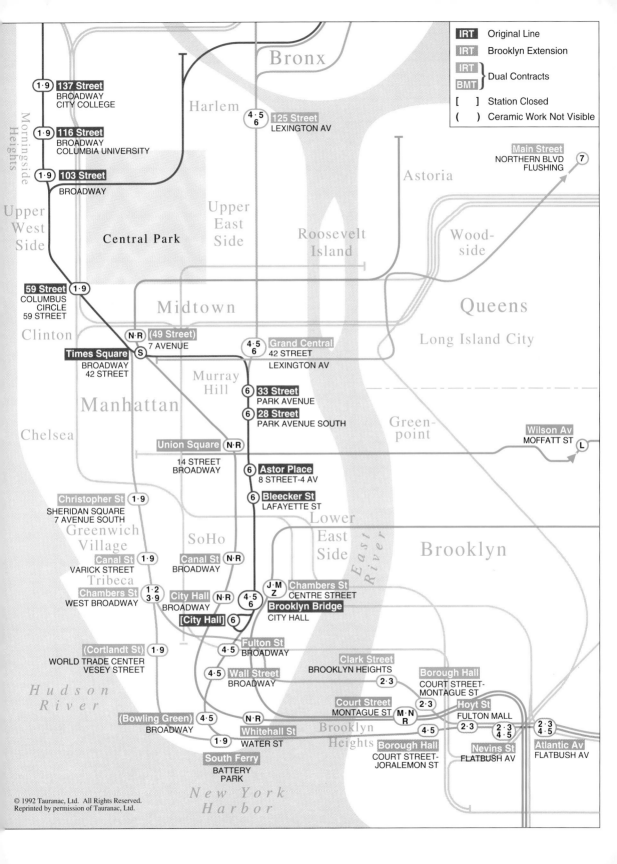

Bronx

Harlem

Morningside Heights

- (1·9) **137 Street**
  BROADWAY
  CITY COLLEGE

- (1·9) **116 Street**
  BROADWAY
  COLUMBIA UNIVERSITY

- (1·9) **103 Street**
  BROADWAY

(4·5 6) **125 Street**
LEXINGTON AV

Astoria

Main Street (7)
NORTHERN BLVD
FLUSHING

Upper
West
Side

Upper
East
Side

Central Park

Roosevelt
Island

Wood-
side

- **59 Street** (1·9)
  COLUMBUS
  CIRCLE
  59 STREET

Midtown

Queens

Clinton

- (N·R) **(49 Street)**
  7 AVENUE

- **Times Square** (S)
  BROADWAY
  42 STREET

Long Island City

(4·5 6) **Grand Central**
42 STREET
LEXINGTON AV

Murray
Hill

Manhattan

- (6) **33 Street**
  PARK AVENUE

- (6) **28 Street**
  PARK AVENUE SOUTH

Green-
point

Chelsea

- **Union Square** (N·R)
  14 STREET
  BROADWAY

- (6) **Astor Place**
  8 STREET-4 AV

Wilson Av (L)
MOFFATT ST

- (6) **Bleecker St**
  LAFAYETTE ST

Lower
East
Side

- **Christopher St** (1·9)
  SHERIDAN SQUARE
  7 AVENUE SOUTH

Greenwich
Village

SoHo

Brooklyn

- **Canal St** (1·9)
  VARICK STREET

Tribeca

- **Canal St** (N·R)
  BROADWAY

East River

- **Chambers St** (1·2 3·9)
  WEST BROADWAY

- **City Hall** (N·R)
  BROADWAY

- (4·5 6)

- (J·M Z) **Chambers St**
  CENTRE STREET

- **Brooklyn Bridge**
  CITY HALL

- **[City Hall]** (6)

- **(Cortland St)** (1·9)
  WORLD TRADE CENTER
  VESEY STREET

- (4·5) **Fulton St**
  BROADWAY

- (4·5) **Wall Street**
  BROADWAY

Clark Street
BROOKLYN HEIGHTS

Borough Hall (2·3)
COURT STREET-
MONTAGUE ST

- **Court Street** (2·3)
  MONTAGUE ST

- **Hoyt St** (2·3)
  FULTON MALL

- **(Bowling Green)** (4·5)
  BROADWAY

- (N·R) **Whitehall St**
  WATER ST

- (1·9)

Borough Hall (M·N R)

Brooklyn
Heights

- (4·5)

- **Borough Hall**
  COURT STREET-
  JORALEMON ST

- **Nevins St** (2·3)
  FLATBUSH AV

- **Atlantic Av** (2·3 4·5)
  FLATBUSH AV

- **South Ferry**
  BATTERY
  PARK

Hudson River

New York Harbor

Legend:
- **IRT** Original Line
- **IRT** Brooklyn Extension
- **IRT** / **BMT** } Dual Contracts
- [ ] Station Closed
- ( ) Ceramic Work Not Visible

INTRODUCTION

The story of New York City's subway is an intricate mosaic.

Take the system that opened on October 27, 1904: the trains were owned and operated by a private company—Interborough Rapid Transit—over tracks and through tunnels which its construction company—Rapid Transit Subway Construction—built for the City; bonds, issued by the City to pay for the construction, were retired by a part of the IRT's revenue; and private investors—especially the IRT's President, August Belmont, Jr.—enjoyed the profit.

That entangling of private with public interests would continue to characterize the system for nearly forty years, just as it had for the previous forty. The idea of underground rapid transit had been debated for at least that many years, and there had been many near-successes, most notably Alfred Beach's plan for a pneumatic system. (In 1870 Beach's elegant prototype actually carried passengers for a year in a block-long tunnel under Broadway, just west of City Hall.) Each of those efforts, including the one which finally gave birth to the 1904 system, involved fierce struggles between competing interests: who should assume the risks? enjoy the profits? determine the routes? own the structures? operate the trains?

Most efforts failed, as Beach's had. But the passenger service that finally began in 1904 has operated continuously for ninety years, evolving into the underground network that serves the City today.

The details of that evolution are too intricate for this book. But a skeleton history may be useful as background to the ceramic work.

The original line (Contract 1—signed February 21, 1900)

At the end of 1899 the City's Rapid Transit Commission asked for bids to build and operate its first underground rapid transit system. The line was to run from City Hall north to Grand Central Station, under 42nd Street to Broadway, and north to 96th Street where the line divided, with western and eastern branches both continuing into the Bronx—a total of 21.19 miles. Of the roughly fifty stations only five, 1½ miles apart, were express stops (Brooklyn Bridge, 14th Street, Grand Central, 72nd Street and 96th Street); the rest were 'way', or local, stations.

John B. McDonald's $35,000,000 bid was accepted by the Commission on January 15, 1900, but he was unable to post the surety bonds required by the City. The financier, August Belmont, Jr., agreed to provide the money but demanded, in return, the right to operate the system. So two companies were born—the Rapid Transit Subway Construction Company (one of the earliest uses of the word 'subway') and the Interborough Rapid Transit Company—both headed by Belmont.

Passenger service began on October 27, 1904, from City Hall to Broadway and 145th Street, and the remaining pieces of the line were opened between November 1904 and August 1908.

The Brooklyn Extension (Contract 2—signed July 21, 1902)

During the construction of the original line the Rapid Transit Commission, prodded by Brooklyn's objection to lack of service, decided to extend express service south from the Brooklyn Bridge station. (The new express tracks bypassed City Hall, which continued as a local stop. At the end of 1945 the station was closed, but the track is still used as a turnaround for local trains.) The work went to the McDonald-Belmont team in an arrangement similar to Contract 1. The line opened to Fulton Street, Wall Street and South Ferry in 1905, and under the East River to Brooklyn's Borough Hall on January 9, 1908. The line was completed to Atlantic Avenue—with great fanfare including a spectacular fireworks display—on May 1, 1908.

Meanwhile the organization of the enterprise had changed again: on July 1, 1907, government control of the subway system was transferred from the City's Rapid Transit Commission to the State's Public Service Commission, District 1.

Dual Contracts (Contracts 3 and 4—signed March 19, 1913)

NOTE: At this point the lines begin to fit, more or less, with present-day names, which are given here in parentheses. The IRT lines are designated by numbers and the BMT by letters starting with 'J'. The IND lines, added later, use the beginning of the alphabet, 'A' through 'G'.

Even as the original line and extension were being built, it became clear that more lines were needed and that the IRT should not be the sole operator. Therefore, after years of discussion as well as an amendment to the State Constitution and enabling legislation, the Dual Contracts were finally signed on March 19, 1913.

Contract 3 was with the IRT. (McDonald and the Rapid Transit Subway Construction Company were by then out of the picture.) It called for several pieces of construction. The first two, often described as 'completing the H', created the lines now commonly called 'the 7th Avenue' and 'the Lexington'.

First, extending the west side of the original line south from Times Square, and adding short extensions to each northern end in the Bronx: From Chambers Street the express lines of the 7th Avenue system ran to Flatbush Avenue/Brooklyn College (#2) and New Lots (#3). The local—#1 (and now #9)—went down to South Ferry, for a time running through a new station on the inside track of the old South Ferry loop station.

Second, extending the east side of the original line north from Grand Central into the Bronx, and adding two southbound extensions out into Brooklyn beyond Atlantic Avenue: This is the present Lexington Avenue line in Manhattan, with extensions to Woodlawn in the Bronx and Utica Avenue in Brooklyn (#4); to 241st Street in the Bronx and Flatbush Avenue/Brooklyn College (#5); and, as the east side local, to Pelham Parkway (#6). (The crossbar of the 'H', between Times Square and Grand Central, began operating as the Shuttle (S) in August, 1918.)

Third, creating a new west-east line that ran parallel to the Shuttle, stopped at the New York Public Library on 5th Avenue, continued under the East River, and ran through Queens to Main Street, Flushing (#7). The river tunnels used by this line are sometimes referred to as 'the Steinway tunnels' after William Steinway who built them at the end of the 19th century for an electric railway, and sometimes as 'the Belmont tunnels' after August Belmont who bought them in 1902. Belmont tried to use them for a passenger line but, by the time he had completed the project in September 1907, he had no valid operating charter. So, after a gala opening—the first passenger run under the East River—the line folded and the tunnels were sealed. Belmont held these white elephants for several years—preferring, understandably, to call them by Steinway's name rather than his own—but finally, in 1913, the City bought them for $3,000,000 as part of Contract 3.

Most of this work was done between 1913 and 1920, but the #7 line did not reach Flushing until 1928.

Contract 4 was with the Brooklyn Rapid Transit Company (BRT), which was transformed in 1923, after five years in receivership, into the Brooklyn Manhattan Transit Corporation (BMT). Construction and operation were handled by subsidiaries, including the New York Municipal Railway Corporation and the New York Consolidated Railroad Company, but the Contract 4 lines were always known as the BRT or, more recently, the BMT.

Contract 4 created a complex network, bringing new underground lines from Queens through Manhattan to Brooklyn, joining there with existing electric and steam lines that made up the BRT's Southern Division. Pieces of that network that figure in the subway ceramics story include:

First, the Broadway/Fourth Avenue line ran from Queensboro Plaza under the East River (originally planned to cross the Queensboro Bridge) through 59th Street to 7th Avenue, and from there south under Broadway to Canal Street. From Canal Street one piece of the line continued south to Whitehall, then under the East River to Montague Street, Brooklyn, and east to DeKalb Avenue. From there the line joined with existing lines of the BRT already serving southern Brooklyn. One of those lines continued down Fourth Avenue (giving the new subway line its name) to 95th Street/Fort Hamilton (R). The Sea Beach line split off at 59th Street, continuing to Coney Island (N).

A second piece of the Contract 4 system left the Broadway line at Canal Street and crossed the Manhattan Bridge to DeKalb Avenue, Brooklyn (not a current route).

A third piece brought a line from the Williamsburg Bridge south through a station under the Municipal Building (Chambers Street), eventually continuing south and into the Whitehall-Montague Street tunnel to Brooklyn (M).

Finally, the 14th Street-Eastern Line began in Manhattan at Sixth Avenue and ran under 14th Street and the East River into Queens, eventually ending at Rockaway Parkway (L).

The IRT and BRT shared track in Queens on the Astoria (N) and Corona (7) lines.

The Independent System (IND)

1925 was the beginning of the end of public-private struggle for construction and operating rights. In that year the City itself started building the last major lines: 'A' through 'G'. These were planned to reach areas not well served by the private IRT and BMT, which had managed to negotiate routes mainly through the most densely populated commercial and residential areas.

Unification (June 1, 1940)

On this date the City, which had always owned the tunnels, tracks and stations, bought the BMT's and IRT's equipment and operating rights for $326,248,000. So the subways were now, for the first time, a fully public system.

Recently there have been short but costly additions, most notably the extension of the 'B' and 'Q' line from 57th Street at Sixth Avenue, under Central Park, 63rd Street and Roosevelt Island, to 21st Street/Queensbridge in western Queens.

And there have been renovations that have changed the appearance of several stations (Bowling Green, Canal Street, Cortlandt Street, 49th Street, 34th Street/Herald Square, etc.), and reconstructions that have tried, often successfully, to preserve or restore original work, Astor Place being an example.

That is far from the full story of the growth of New York's subway system. New York City and transit historians have written many volumes. The purpose here was only to provide a backdrop for the story of the subway ceramics: the mosaic signs, bas relief emblems and terra cotta friezes which enrich and guide our travels.

The story of the most significant ceramic work falls in a period of less than twenty years: from the height of the Arts and Crafts movement at the turn of the century to the end of World War I. It divides into two phases:

1. *The original subway and its extension to Brooklyn*   All of the ceramic work of this period was designed by the architectural firm of Heins and LaFarge, consulting architects to the Rapid Transit Commission.

2. *The Dual Contracts lines*   Here the design work was by several artists under the direction of Squire J. Vickers, the designing architect of the Public Service Commission.

This book will be divided in the same way, with a brief history and photographs in each section.

HEINS AND LA FARGE
The Original Lines

The railway and its equipment as contemplated by the contract constitute a great public work. All parts of the structure where exposed to public sight shall therefore be designed, constructed, and maintained with a view to the beauty of their appearance, as well as to their efficiency.

—*Rapid Transit Commission contract, 1900*

With those words William Barclay Parsons, Chief Engineer of the Rapid Transit Commission, ensured that New York's subway would be different from its European predecessors. The subway was being created during a time of rapid developments in technology and changing tastes in art. Parsons was mindful of those pulls and determined, as the contract language shows, to find a resolution—a way of achieving art *and* utility.

In architecture these were exciting times. New technologies and materials, including reinforced concrete, were making possible structures unimaginable only a short time before. Though trained as an engineer, Parsons appreciated the architectural aspects of his project. Perhaps his most important insight was in seeing the subway as a *structure* rather than just a utilitarian tunnel—a horizontal 'building', as deserving of coherent architecture as the buildings then beginning to fill the City's sky.

Art was in a period of transition, too—near the peak of the Arts and Crafts movement, but with the modernism of the 1913 Armory Show only a dozen years away. Given the interest at that time in bringing art to a broader public, Parsons must have seen the subway stations as an opportunity. And he could not have found better collaborators than George C. Heins and Christopher Grant LaFarge.

Heins and LaFarge were respected architects already doing important work that included the Cathedral of St. John the Divine and several buildings at the new Bronx Zoo. In addition to those credentials, they were brother-in-law and son of John LaFarge—muralist, stained glass designer and leader in the Arts and Crafts movement in the United States. The LaFarge name alone would have given the son a kind of prominence, but he had inherited his father's sense of color and design and was a leader, in his own right, in the revival of decorative arts. Recognizing their value as allies, Parsons chose them as architectural advisors. They were paid an annual fee of $2,500, a bargain even at 1901 rates!

Their assignment—to design the stations—was not easy. They needed to find a way to bring pleasure and reassurance into a bleak tunnel, and a way to let the passengers know which of these basically similar stations their train had just arrived in. A further challenge was that many of those passengers would be recent immigrants who did not read English.

Heins and LaFarge had to work fast, since construction was well under way by the time they were appointed on March 7, 1901. Because they lacked design examples from the existing underground systems (Paris, London, Budapest and Boston), they seem to have relied on the model they knew best: their own work at the Zoo. They carried several techniques from that project into the subway. These included Guastavino arches and vaulted ceilings, polychrome tile, and ornamental figures: elephant, hippopotamus and rhinoceros at the Zoo; eagles, boats and beavers in the subway. Their challenge was to create in each station distinctive design and appropriate ornament: 'signs', verbal or artistic, which together would please and inform the passengers.

The City Hall station, with its single track on a tight loop, offered Heins and LaFarge a unique opportunity. Their success there was recognized at the time by an effusive writer in *House and Garden* who described the "apotheosis of curves" and continued:

The broad structural vaults satisfy the esthetic and scientific imagination that a necessary strength has been created underground in the proximity of the Postoffice and the skyscrapers of Park Row. Moreover the sturdy forms here and the restraint of ornament are suited to the workaday heart of 'downtown', where the daily rider will be quickly swung to his office on these smooth curves and as gaily spirited away.

But City Hall set an impossible standard. Everywhere else Heins and LaFarge would be faced with right angles and straight platforms in wide stations, forcing them to rely entirely on a limited variety of surface treatments. They used conventional materials— marble, brick, and ceramic or glass tile—which were durable enough to withstand dampness and frequent scrubbing. Also available were the ancient technique of decorative mosaic and the relatively new one of architectural terra cotta. There was variety, too, in the decorative motifs they used: egg and dart moldings, key and swastika borders, scrolls, bells, rosettes, leaves, garlands, cornucopias and wreaths reminiscent of Della Robia. The choice of these traditional patterns and designs was perhaps part of a conscious effort by the architects to surround passengers with the familiar, hoping to ease their anxiety at being underground.

Another part of that effort was the decision to work with designers and producers of ceramics who were comfortable with a vocabulary of conventional images. The two most prominent were the Grueby Faience Company of Boston and the Rookwood Pottery of Cincinnati. Originally art potteries producing mostly tiles and vases, both firms became involved in architectural faience work at the turn of the century. It is not entirely certain which details of the designs were provided by the architects and which were left to the potteries, nor which pottery was responsible for each of the ceramics. But there seems to be rough agreement on who ultimately produced many of them. Herbert Peck, in *The Book of Rookwood* (1968), notes that Rookwood's records for 1903 show a "large contract" of "$5,659 for furnishing the decorative faience for the 23rd, 79th, 86th and 91st Street stations of the New York City subway." Rookwood's architectural department continued to grow, boosted by the contract for the somewhat later large plaques at Wall Street and Fulton Street. The Grueby Faience Company was responsible for many of the distinctive early plaques: the ship at Columbus Circle, the eagle at 33rd Street, the beaver at Astor Place and a similar plaque for 50th Street, wreath-like medallions at 116th Street and 14th Street (now hidden), and the blue oval sign at Bleecker Street. Grueby also seems to have created the heavy-bordered name panel at 28th Street and smaller number and letter signs and medallions at Brooklyn Bridge, 18th Street (now closed), 42nd Street, 103rd Street and 110th Street.

Both Rookwood and Grueby produced faience, an opaque glazed ceramic which is fired twice (as opposed to single-fired terra cotta) and can achieve a greater range of colors. Another supplier of ceramic signs and ornament was the Atlantic Terra Cotta Company which joined the project after Grueby and Rookwood—brought in perhaps because costs needed to be controlled and their terra cotta was less expensive than the others' faience. They were responsible for shield-like cartouches at Canal Street, Worth Street (now closed), Spring Street and Third Avenue in the Bronx. Atlantic Terra Cotta also produced small number panels for several stations on the west side line. They were done by ingenious mass-production: a standard plaque, bordered with cornucopias, was designed to receive a separately molded panel with the street number of the station on it. Examples can be seen in several stations including 86th Street, 137th Street (page 41), 145th Street and 157th Street.

Most of the ceramic work produced under the direction of Heins and LaFarge can still be seen and appreciated ninety years after it was done. LaFarge, in a report to Parsons, summarized their accomplishment modestly:

We have used a very limited number of different materials, rather few patterns and not many colors. These we have combined and recombined in varying arrangements, so as to produce a pretty considerable appearance of diversity, and all this has been for the distinct and proper purpose of aiding the traveler in the rapid and easy identification of his whereabouts.

Did they achieve Parsons' goal of 'beauty and efficiency'? Most of the work, artistically, was dignified and elegant. Where it perhaps was less successful was in "aiding the traveler in the rapid and easy identification of his whereabouts." Clear station identification needs less intricate design and better placement of visual clues than they achieved in some of the stations. (Apparently the designers soon recognized these failings. In later stations, south of Brooklyn Bridge, identification is clearer. The Fulton Street, Wall Street and South Ferry picture emblems are larger, more colorful and generally less high on the wall.)

But Heins and LaFarge's basic idea of using art to carry information was sound. Critics question the idea that beavers or sailboats could help riders identify stations. What immigrant would know about Astor's beaver trade? Who would know that the boat at 59th Street was the flagship of that earlier immigrant whose name was given to the intersection above? The new immigrant would not—and neither would most native New Yorkers. But all of them would come to know the symbols. The beavers can be read as easily as a barber's pole: you know you are at Astor Place.

Heins and LaFarge used a variety of materials and design elements in the stations. The IRT's commemorative book described them this way:

The ceilings are separated into panels by wide ornamental mouldings, and the panels are decorated with narrower mouldings and rosettes. The bases of the walls are buff Norman brick. Above this is glass tile or glazed tile, and above the tile is a faience or terra-cotta cornice. Ceramic mosaic is used for decorative panels, friezes, pilasters and name tablets. A different decorative treatment is used at each station, including a distinctive color scheme. At some stations the number of the intersecting street, or initial letter of the street name, is shown on conspicuous plaques, at other stations the number or letter is in the panel. At some stations artistic emblems have been used in the scheme of decoration, as at Astor Place, the beaver; at Columbus Circle, the great navigator's Caravel; at 116th Street, the seal of Columbia University.

Much of the decorative and sign work, both faience and terra cotta, is heavier than in the later stations done under Vickers in the teens and twenties. In fact, all of the bas relief plaques, elaborate Della Robia-like medallions, and molded terra cotta friezes belong to the Heins and LaFarge period.

This 1974 view of the Astor Place station confirms the IRT's description and gives a good sense of the relation between plaques, name panels and other decorative elements. The plaques here are 22½ by 14 inches. They were set at 15-foot intervals, with name panels at strategic points between. This is typical of the stations of Contracts 1 and 2.

City Hall   October 27, 1904   IRT   (closed December 31, 1945)

The City Hall station is one of the most written about yet least seen, since it has been closed for nearly fifty years. But in 1904 it was the City's pride and joy, the flagship station of the long-awaited subway system. Located on a loop of single track, the station presented Parsons and Heins and LaFarge unique design possibilities, and they used them to full advantage: the platform and track could be bridged by a single snug arch; the Guastavinos' special system of setting tiles in a criss-cross pattern with fast-setting mortar created lightweight, centerless vaults; those, in turn, permitted vault lights of amethyst glass, allowing daylight to supplement the light from elegant chandeliers; and, because of the depth of the station, ticket booths could be located on a mezzanine level reached by two arched stairways from the street, leaving the platform clear for passengers. Most of the station's special character is in the structure itself, but there are ornamental elements too: the arches and vault ribs are edged with colored tile, and there are name plaques on the walls and over the stairway from the platform.

It is a shame that this Landmark station, now used as a turnaround loop for local trains, can be seen today only on occasional historic tours. But there are similar Guastavino arches visible above the Brooklyn Bridge station, in the corner of McKim, Mead and White's Municipal Building. And grander examples can be seen at the Cathedral of St. John the Divine, St. Paul's Chapel at Columbia University, Ellis Island and the Elephant House at the Bronx Zoo.

◄ A NOTE ABOUT THE PICTURE CAPTIONS: Next to the name of each station is the date when it was opened for passengers, followed by one or more numbers (IRT) or letters (BMT) showing present line designations. The color bar underlining that information uses the colors from the map (page 7) to show which contract the station was built under.

This was a significant station, being the most southern of the five express stops on the original line. But its clever 'ꓭB' monogram notwithstanding, it lacks the kind of distinctive, coherent design found at some lesser stations like Astor Place and Bleecker Street. The square Grueby panel with the double-B, set on top of a mosaic pilaster, is identical to the '14' and '42' at 14th Street and Times Square; the mosaic name panel—only one remains, on the darkened platform south of the control booth—is like those in many other stations; and the large eagles, visible in early photographs but now covered, were identical to those at 14th Street (also gone) and 33rd Street. The station became even more undistinguished when it was extended northward in the early sixties, almost merging with the Worth Street station which was then closed.

The double-B emblems may be seen on the eastern wall of the mezzanine, near the station entrance at the Municipal Building. Opposite, on the western wall, there are three bronze plaques which were moved there from City Hall after that station closed. The two smaller, rectangular ones commemorate the Rapid Transit Subway Construction Company and the staff of the Rapid Transit Commission's Chief Engineer, William Barclay Parsons. The largest, curved to fit City Hall's Guastavino arches, celebrates "The First Municipal Rapid Transit Railroad...Suggested by the Chamber of Commerce...Authorized by the State...Constructed by the City."

The station takes its name from the street above, named for an early Dutch landowner. The bold, oval name plaques are unique in size, shape and color, but their heavy, ornate borders are typical of Heins and LaFarge's designs. Each large plaque is composed of twenty-seven faience pieces. They were made by the Grueby Faience Company of Boston and are now protected as New York City Landmarks.

In addition to the large signs—four on each platform—there are smaller emblems, in the same brilliant blue, with tulips whose leaves wrap around a sinuous 'B'. There also are blue and white mosaic signs, added when platforms were extended to accommodate longer trains, and a third generation of more modern signs with letters glazed onto larger tiles, some with the name abbreviated to 'Bl'ker'.

One of the most beloved station emblems, the industrious beaver, represents an early source of John Jacob Astor's wealth: beaver pelts. The strong design, vivid colors and large size of the plaques—22½ by 14 inches, plus 8-10 inch borders—make them unusually effective in identifying the station.

An extensive restoration of the Landmark station was completed in 1986. The walls and beavers were refurbished, and dramatic new porcelain enamel panels, created by Milton Glaser, were added. His panels repeat many of the colors and design elements of the Grueby beaver plaques, especially the brick-red diamonds at the upper corners.

Outside the station there is a new cast-iron entrance house identical to the originals built by the Hecla Iron Works. These had been used at many IRT stations, but, because all of them were destroyed during the fifties, the Astor Place replica is the sole reminder of that elegant era.

The station at 50th Street (7th Avenue) is marked by a Grueby plaque identical to Astor Place's in size, color and ornate border. But, lacking an apt symbol like the beaver, the center panel simply shows a large, straightforward '50'.

The massive sign here is one of the largest. It is done in Grueby faience with an unusually heavy border in a fret motif. Only two of these signs are left on each platform. (On the uptown platform there is a third sign: a mosaic replica of the originals, presumably done to replace one that was destroyed. Its lettering gives it a quite modern look.)

High on the wall there are several pairs of '28' medallions, probably also by Grueby. They are similar to medallions at 103rd Street, but those are set singly and are larger.

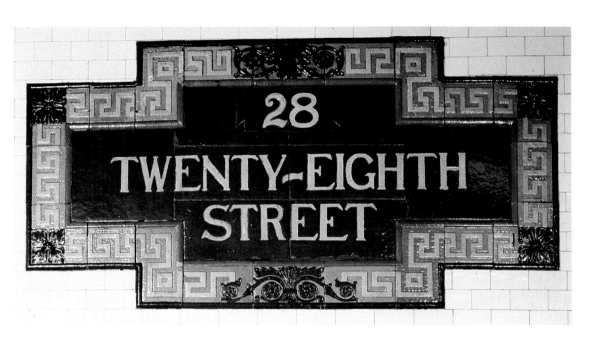

The dramatic Grueby faience eagles made a clear connection with the 71st Regiment Armory that stood above the station. The original 1892 armory burned in 1902. Its replacement (now also gone) was built at the same time as the subway, so the eagle was a natural symbol for Heins and LaFarge to choose.

Each eagle is made up of seven elements: the solid central shield gripped by the eagle's talons, and six border pieces: head, tail and two divided wings. *House and Garden*, in 1904, applauded the "vigor and large scale of this ornament," but went on to note that "its special application to the Thirty-Third Street Station is destroyed by its mysterious appearance also at Fourteenth Street"—and, according to early photographs, at Brooklyn Bridge too. But those errant eagles have disappeared from view, so the ones at 33rd Street now, finally, are "special." They are protected as New York City Landmarks.

Around 1925, two mosaic eagles were added on the northbound side when that side of Park Avenue was raised and widened and station entrances were reconfigured.

Longacre Square was given a new name at the same time that it acquired a subway. Adolph S. Ochs had just gained a controlling interest in *The New York Times* and was building a new headquarters for the paper in the center of the square. So August Belmont wrote to Alexander Orr, Chairman of the Rapid Transit Commission, suggesting that the subway station use the name "Times Square." The Commission approved. On December 31, 1904, two months after the subway opened, the *Times* moved into its new building, with elaborate fireworks providing the Square's first New Year's Eve celebration. (Perhaps to return Belmont's favor, the *Times* was always generous in its praise, hailing Belmont when he died as "the Father of the subways.")

Times Square began as a local stop. The station was in the curve of the original line as it swung from 42nd Street under Broadway. But in 1913 the City contracted with the IRT to extend the east side of the original line north from Grand Central and the west side south from Times Square. The track from Grand Central to Times Square thus became the Shuttle.

The large name panels in the Times Square station were among the most ornate mosaic signs in the system. The same design was used at Borough Hall (1908) and, according to early photographs, at 14th Street, though none is visible there today. Only three remain at Times Square. Two are at the west end of the northern Shuttle platform, on either side of the token booth, and one is at the east end of the southern Shuttle platform. (Near it is a door topped by a terra cotta "Knickerbocker," installed in 1906 for John Jacob Astor's new Knickerbocker Hotel.)

Columbus Circle is identified by a jaunty ship sailing before the wind on a wavy, blue-green sea—a classic Arts and Crafts motif. *House and Garden*, in 1904, called the ships "the galleys of Columbus," and the IRT's commemorative book referred to "the great navigator's Caravel." Many since then have called it the Santa Maria, though that ship was likely a 'nao': larger than a caravel, with a topsail in addition to the mainsails and staysail. But, whatever the name or type of ship, the symbol has for ninety years helped passengers make the Columbus connection.

The decorative work at Columbus Circle is interesting for its variety. Apparently it was one of the first stations ready for ceramic installations, so the Grueby Faience Company used it as a place to test different kinds of work. Early photographs suggest there were two kinds of name panel: one faience and the other mosaic. None of the faience remains and only a few of the mosaic.

The cornice is elaborate, as is the setting for each ship plaque: a wide border of rosettes joined by pieces of nautical line; and a bas relief swag draped below. The ship itself is done in such heavy relief that its prow actually thrusts out of the plaque, conveying depth and motion. (The same is true of the sloops at South Ferry.)

Much of the ceramic work has been damaged or destroyed, but what remains is protected by Landmark status.

35

103rd Street   October 27, 1904   IRT

These handsome medallions, probably the work of the Grueby Faience Company, are placed high on the wall—too high to be easily seen from the train. The more visible identification is a classic IRT name panel of the design used at Hoyt, Spring and 110th Streets and at many other stations.

116th Street / Columbia University October 27, 1904 IRT ①

This is one of the few stations where it still is possible to see two different emblems: a wreath with the number 116, and a wreath encircling the seal of Columbia. There are heavy swastika borders around the emblems and a faience torch on each side.

All of this elaborate Grueby work is unusually high on the wall, making it difficult for passengers to see. The more useful clues in this station are the Columbia-blue tile borders running along the walls and bordering the eye-level name panels. (All of the attention to Columbia, in symbol, words and color, may be because Parsons, the Chief Engineer, was a Trustee of the University.)

The station became a Landmark in 1979.

137th Street / City College   October 27, 1904   IRT ① ⑨

The most eye-catching symbol here is the large name panel in City College lavender. Above the name is the bas relief seal of the College, representing past, present and future. The color, size and unique design of these signs made them effective identification, but a recent renovation has covered all but one on each platform. The renovation also concealed interesting '137' plaques of green terra cotta. They were made by the Atlantic Terra Cotta Company using one mold for the cornucopia frame and another for the number-panel insert. The frames were produced in large quantity and used, with different number panels, for several stations. Though gone from 137th Street, they can still be seen in other west side stations at 86th, 145th, and 157th Streets.

Fulton Street   January 16, 1905   IRT ④ ⑤

Though Robert Fulton did not invent the steamboat, he was the first—with Robert Livingston's backing—to show that it could be financially successful. His "North River Steam Boat" made its maiden voyage in 1807. It later was referred to as the "Clermont" after the Hudson River landing Livingston offered for its use.

The plaque commemorating this, and marking the street that bears Fulton's name, was made by the Rookwood Pottery. It is one of three—with Wall Street and South Ferry—of this unusually ornate design: a large plaque draped with garlands, with an initial in a plaque below.

There are four of these on the southbound platform. They are protected as New York City Landmarks.

Wall Street　　　　　　　　　　June 12, 1905　　　　　　　　　　IRT　④　⑤

Like its twin at Fulton Street, the Wall Street plaque was made by Rookwood Pottery. Also like Fulton Street it is an intricate scene, different from the simpler plaques of Contract 1: an eagle, a ship, a beaver. Here there is a sense of a foreground with grass and trees, a Dutch house in the background, and the wall in between. It is a north view of the wall which protected the northern edge of the settlement of Nieuw Amsterdam.

Much of the ceramic work in the Wall Street station has been restored and is protected as a Landmark.

The coved station walls at Bowling Green made it impossible to install the massive, ornate plaques used in the other Manhattan stations of Contract 2: Fulton Street, Wall Street and South Ferry. So Heins and LaFarge created a unique solution, alternating mosaic name panels with elegant mosaic tapestries.

Unfortunately, this fine and unusual work was lost when the station was refurbished in the seventies, though similar mosaic 'hangings' are still visible at 72nd Street/Broadway and 110th Street/Lenox Avenue. The walls at Bowling Green are now a solid, vivid orange, as in the 49th Street station. (The reconstruction at Bowling Green took twice as long and cost half as much, in unadjusted dollars, as the construction of the entire original line!)

The station is named for Bowling Green—the oldest existing public park in New York City. The entrance house there was removed in the reconstruction, but one remains in Battery Park at the southern end of the station. Designed by Heins and LaFarge, it is now a New York City Landmark. (Another, also a Landmark, is at the 72nd Street/Broadway station.)

South Ferry   July 10, 1905   IRT (1) (9)

Many have said that the South Ferry plaque—a sloop sailing the green waters of the harbor beneath banked clouds and a blue sky, with a festoon of garlands and a monogram below— is the most splendid of all the ceramic works. The number and size of the plaques (fifteen of them, 14 by 23 inches) certainly create a dramatic effect. And the effect is heightened by the curve of the platform: following the tip of the island, it gives a feeling of being surrounded by ships.

The station has a complex history:
• The Contract 2 line to Brooklyn had a spur with a double-track loop under the Battery. The South Ferry station was on the outer track.
• In 1909 a two-car shuttle was added for extra service between Bowling Green and South Ferry.
• In 1918, when the west side line was extended south from Times Square, with the local trains running beyond Chambers Street to South Ferry, a platform was added on the loop's inside track which until then had been used for midday storage of trains. The new platform was identified by a mosaic frieze with the initials 'SF' set in a hexagonal design similar to most other stations on that new line.
• Finally, when east side service to South Ferry was discontinued in the mid-seventies, the west side locals were moved to the highly decorated outside track.

Borough Hall   January 9, 1908   IRT

The elaborate decoration at Borough Hall celebrates the subway's arrival in Brooklyn just ten years after Brooklyn joined New York City. There are very large and intricate name panels, almost identical to those at Times Square, and wide mosaic panels hanging like tapestries. At intervals along the top of the wall, set in a deep mosaic frieze, are heavy bas relief wreaths with a 'BH' monogram in the center. Susan Tunick's research indicates that, like the plaques at South Ferry, they are the work of the Hartford Faience Company and that the mosaic versions on the platforms' extensions are by the American Encaustic Tiling Company. There has been a major restoration of this station, the only one in Brooklyn with Landmark protection.

Hoyt Street   May 1, 1908   IRT (2) (3)

The name panels are typical of those in many of the early stations: a central colored panel with the station name, usually in white letters, surrounded by a mosaic border with small, square extensions at the upper corners.

The blue of the border at Hoyt Street is similar to the blue at 116th Street/Columbia University; but there, instead of four tulips in each corner 'tab', there are symbols of learning: a book and a lamp.

A few original name panels remain on each platform, survivors of a renovation that covered much of the station with beige tile.

Nevins Street   May 1, 1908   IRT   ④ ⑤

The elaborate mosaic sign is larger than most, and the format is unusual. (The 168th Street station is similar in design.)

Only a few complete name panels remain on each platform at Nevins Street. Because they have suffered serious water damage, most will not be saved in a current rehabilitation project. One panel, though, will be preserved in offices below the station.

A few classic IRT name panels survive at Atlantic Avenue, as well as these emblems of an 'A' flanked by tulips. There are similar emblems at several other stations including Spring, Bleecker and 110th Streets, and at the closed Worth Street station; but each has a slightly different flower or ribbon design. (The Spring Street station has been beautifully restored.)

What is particularly interesting here is the two generations of 'A's. The 1910 contract for platform extensions specified that "the new work shall harmonize with the station of which it is to form a part." The result was the faithful reproduction, in mosaic, of the original terra cotta emblems. Similar reproductions can be seen at Borough Hall on the Lexington Avenue line.

At street level is one of the few remaining Heins and LaFarge entrance houses. But it has been out of use for some years and is so deteriorated and disfigured that, except at roof level, it is almost unrecognizable. The two other remaining entrance houses are protected by Landmark status: at 72nd Street/Broadway and in Battery Park at the Bowling Green station.

The drawings for this station were completed by Heins and LaFarge on May 9, 1907, just before they finished their work as consulting architects to the Rapid Transit Commission. (The Commission's authority was transferred to the State's new Public Service Commission on July 1, 1907.)

The station was to have been part of a loop connecting a line from the Williamsburg Bridge with another running over the Brooklyn Bridge, which accounts for the 'Brooklyn Bridge' name panel on the drawings. That loop connection was never made, but in 1913—after the Dual Contracts were signed—the line over the Williamsburg Bridge was continued from Essex Street to this station, which was then named 'Chambers Street'. Much later (1931) the line was tied into the Whitehall-Montague Street (Brooklyn) tunnel and carried trains on what is now the M line.

The large, squat, T-shaped plaques are each centered on a pink marble pilaster. They show the Manhattan pier of the Brooklyn Bridge, but without any of the cables sweeping gracefully, as they do on the bridge, away from the tower. The bridge is silhouetted against billowing clouds, with small boats and the Statue of Liberty beyond. The 1913 execution of these plaques is faithful to Heins and LaFarge's design, but, consistent with work designed under Vickers, the relief is less heavy than in its twins at Wall Street, Fulton Street and South Ferry. The station is thus a sort of bridge between the Heins and LaFarge period in which it was designed and the Vickers era in which it was executed.

Eight of these plaques—five of which can be seen easily—remain on an unused platform across the Queens-bound tracks of the J,M & Z line, reached from the northeast end of the Brooklyn Bridge IRT station.

SQUIRE J. VICKERS
The Dual Contracts

Shortly before Heins and LaFarge ended their work as consulting architects to the Rapid Transit Commission, a young architect began a career there that would continue for 36 years. It was a career that started before the opening of the IRT's Brooklyn extension and continued through the building of the IRT/BMT Dual System and the City's IND lines and two years beyond the unification into one public system—a truly impressive span of rapid transit history (during all of which the fare never changed from a nickel!). The architect was Squire J. Vickers. His name is not as well known as those of Heins and LaFarge, yet he played the same role in the design and finish of the Dual Contracts stations as they had for the earlier contracts.

Vickers was born on an upstate farm in 1872. After high school he worked as a teacher to earn money for college and, in his mid-twenties, went to Cornell. There he studied architecture and began lifelong friendships with two other architecture students: Jay Van Everen and Herbert Dole. After graduating in 1900 he came to New York and worked in Dole's private architectural practice. Three years later he went to work for the Board of Education and, in 1906, for the Rapid Transit Commission where he stayed for the rest of his career. (Actually, authority over the subway system was transferred from the City to the State in 1907, and back to the City in 1924; so his employment shifted from the City's Rapid Transit Commission to the State's Public Service—later 'Transit'—Commission, and in 1924 back to the City under a Board of Transportation.)

When the time came to design the stations of the Dual Contracts lines, there was no need for Alfred Craven, the Commission's Chief Engineer, to hire outside architects as Parsons had earlier. Vickers was on his staff and an experienced chief architect. He had taken over all of the design work after Heins and LaFarge left in 1907 and was well able now to take responsibility for the stations of the new lines.

In addition to professional experience, Vickers had several qualities that turned out to be important: as a student of history he was respectful of the past, yet he was not bound by it. Years later he described the materials used by Heins and LaFarge as "durable and colorful, reflecting light and cheerfulness," and he acknowledged that "this was the heritage we accepted in 1906." But he went on to enumerate the many ways his team had reinterpreted that legacy. Also underlying his work was respect for structure and for honesty of design: "Massive walls of concrete and steel on every side give evidence of great strength and utility. We felt that any attempt to hide the structure or conceal its strength would be wrong; we also felt that the decoration must have an element of severeness and restraint." Finally, quite independent of his subway work, he had a longstanding interest in ornamental treatment of architectural surfaces and had experimented, on his own, with carved friezes and mosaics. He was also a serious painter whose work was the subject of a retrospective exhibit at New York's Shepherd Gallery in 1992.

His influence is unmistakable in the Dual Contracts stations:

• The way they are identified is simple and clean: name panels are rectangular, without elaborate borders or garlands; the historic plaques are set in rectangular or hexagonal frames, never curved. The art work in the plaques may be intricately detailed, but the settings are quite plain.

• None of the historic plaques is in relief, nor any of the station initials, number plaques or decorative borders. Everything has a smooth surface and is set flush with the wall.

• There are no eagles, beavers or locomotives in the plaques. Instead, there are scenes, usually of buildings. And the scenes seem always to have been faithfully copied from real life or old photographs or paintings.

• Mosaic work in both friezes and plaques is very colorful, with greater variety of color than was used in the earlier faience and terra cotta. And the color is used in fanciful ways, not limited to green trees, blue skies and white clouds.

• But, among stations, there is less variety of approach than in the earlier work of Heins and LaFarge. A Vickers station, generally, has a less distinctive 'signature'.

The materials used in these stations included mosaic similar to the earlier period, but a special technique was used to produce and set it. Here is Vickers' description:

…The mosaic was of the cut variety, that is, the body is burned in strips, glazed, and then broken into irregular squares. The designs are set by hand and shipped in sections with paper pasted on the front. These sections set against the wall flush with the tile. In certain stations the color bands and name tablets are a combination of mosaic and hand-made tile.

Another kind of mass-production may have been used in the late teens to create 'mosaic' plaques like the small ones on the 7th Avenue line at Christopher, Canal and Cortlandt Streets. Herman Mueller was a New Jersey tile manufacturer who probably produced some of those plaques. Anticipating later work, he wrote to Vickers about "something new"—simulated mosaics. "The small parts are made or produced by making larger pieces and separating the surface pieces by deep grooves which are afterwards filled up with mortar. This makes the assembling and setting easy and work of this class can be done at 1/2 to 1/3 of the cost when the small particles are assembled."

It is clear that Vickers oversaw all of the design work and had a strong hand in choosing the materials to be used. He undoubtedly decided which stations would have historic plaques, perhaps choosing the subject as well as guiding the design. It is not clear which plaques are entirely his own work, but it is likely that several are.*

We do know that at least four were done by Vickers' Cornell friend, Jay Van Everen, who was then painting in New York. They had remained close over the years, and Van Everen came often to visit Vickers, a widower who lived with his daughter, Ruth, in Grand View on Hudson. She remembered years later how her father and "Uncle Bill," as she called Van Everen, would work together creating whimsical garden ornaments or applying bits of tile to concrete surfaces and wooden beams on the porch and in her father's studio.

In his painting Van Everen was influenced by Synchromist painters who were experimenting with unconventional use of color. That influence is clear in his subway designs, with their fancifully-colored boats and roofs and clouds and steeples. Curiously, there is no official record of Van Everen's designs for the subway. Yet there is clear evidence that he created four plaques: 14th Street/Union Square and Canal Street on the BMT; 125th Street and Clark Street on the IRT. (All of these are pictured here.) There is also, at the Whitney Museum, a Van Everen oil study of the Metropolitan Life tower, but the plaque never appeared in the 23rd Street BMT station for which it was designed.

Another of the designers was Vickers' Cornell friend Herbert Dole, who eventually came to work for Vickers at the Public Service Commission. Vickers credited him with "most" of the historic plaques. He designed the small hexagonal plaques set in fine mosaic bands at Christopher and Canal Streets, as well as the far bolder plaque at Borough Hall on the 7th Avenue. That versatility suggests that he might also have designed the plaques at Whitehall and Court Street. Or perhaps those were Vickers' work.

Given the quantity and quality of his work, it is puzzling that Vickers has remained so obscure. Perhaps that is because he was not brought in from the outside with fanfare, as Heins and LaFarge had been. He was already at the Transit Commission, working quietly in the system. But his obscurity probably has more to do with his unassuming personality and manner. He seems to have had little interest in making a name for himself. He was an artist who was rewarded by enjoyment of what he created. And he delighted in sharing that pleasure with the subway riders of New York.

*Although it is not discussed in this book, considerable ceramic work was applied to the concrete surfaces of stations on the elevated pieces of the system. That work was almost entirely Vickers' design.

In a paper Vickers presented to the Society of Municipal Engineers in February, 1933, he described the design and construction of the Dual Contracts stations.

By placing all wall materials in one plane, unsanitary dust-catching ledges were eliminated.... To reduce expenses, low cement bases were substituted for the more elaborate marble and brick bases used in the original stations.

By the elimination of pilasters and panels in the tile-work, a wainscot of tile about 7 feet high was laid through out the length of the station, unbroken except for such natural breaks as doorways, stairs, etc., thereby effecting a considerable saving in the setting of the tile.

Above the tile was placed a band of cut mosaic executed in color and in simple geometric design. These bands usually have initial letters or figures at the bent points to help passengers in the trains identify the stations. In twenty of the stations historic plaques of colored faience are inserted instead of initial letters,... plaques which nudge the memory to recall the past.

These walls, therefore, from the standpoint of economy, sanitation and simplicity are, we think, an improvement over the walls of the original stations.

Simplification and uniformity, of both design and materials, were the hallmarks of the Vickers stations. The 1919 Borough Hall station shown here is a good example.

Christopher Street / Sheridan Square   July 1, 1918   IRT ①

Christopher Street is one of three stations with small hexagonal picture plaques set within a mosaic frieze. The plaques are only 10 by 10 inches. Their pastel colors may seem an odd choice, given the subject: the old State penitentiary at the foot of West 10th Street, demolished when Sing Sing Prison was built. But the overall effect is pleasing.

The work, both here and at Canal Street, bears strong resemblance to Van Everen's work. But it is said that both were designed by Herbert Dole.

Canal Street   July 1, 1918   IRT ① ⑨

St. John's Chapel of Trinity Church stood for over a hundred years on Varick Street facing Hudson Square. Despite careful efforts to save it when the street was widened during construction for the subway, it had to be torn down in 1918.

The small ceramic plaque shows, remarkably accurately, the towering spire which in the 1800's was a landmark in the City's skyline.

The plaque seems to have been designed by Herbert Dole, an architect under Squire Vickers at the Public Service Commission.

Chambers Street   July 1, 1918   IRT (1) (2) (3) (9)

In 1754 Kings College was founded under a royal charter. From then until 1857 it was in downtown Manhattan on land bounded by Barclay, Church and Murray Streets and West Broadway. This plaque shows a narrowed version of the College's original building, with two robed students coming down the path. At the time of independence from England the college changed its name to Columbia College. In 1857 it moved to 49th and Madison and, in 1897— just before the subway came—to Morningside Heights.

It is the only institution celebrated in two subway stations: here and at 116th Street.

Cortlandt Street July 1, 1918 IRT (1) (9)

Long after the ferry stopped running from Cortlandt Street to Paulus Hook (Jersey City), ceramic ferry boats sailed along the subway platform walls. But now they, too, are gone—a casualty of the station renovation at the time the World Trade Center was built.

This cheerful small plaque is identical in size and shape to those still at Canal Street and Christopher Street. It is possible that Herbert Dole, credited with those plaques, designed this one as well. But the building-like elements of the ferryboat are so reminiscent of the fantasy buildings and towers in Squire Vickers' paintings that this plaque may well be his own design.

71

Clark Street/Brooklyn Heights   April 15, 1919   IRT ② ③

This is the largest of the subway's mosaic plaques: 28 by 13 inches, set in a heavy border of sea-green tile. The long vertical shape is ideal for depicting Brooklyn Heights above and the then-busy East River docks below.

The identity of the artist, Jay Van Everen, is documented by a duplicate plaque in the Whitney Museum's collection. As in much of Van Everen's work, the forms are realistic and the colors fanciful.

Most of the plaques are across the tracks on the curved walls of the tunnels, but two are on the wall at the east end of the platform.

The station entrance is inside the arcade of the St. George Hotel, at the corner of Clark and Henry Streets. The 1914 architect's drawing gives Henry Street as the station's name.

The name panel and historic plaque at Borough Hall are exemplary. The designs are clean and the colors bold. In the name panel and frieze, occasional bits of bright yellow, hand-made tile help define the borders. Within the plaque, billowing clouds set the cupola off from the deep blue sky. (It was typical of the Vickers-Van Everen-Dole design team to portray a building that no longer existed. Borough Hall still stands, but the cupola here is the original, taller one destroyed by fire in 1895.) One of the architectural drawings for the station seems to indicate that Dole was the designer.

This is the perfect place to see the difference between the Heins and LaFarge and the Vickers stations. A passageway connects the two Borough Hall stations. The distance is short, but the difference is dramatic. They were built just eleven years apart.

Grand Central   July 17, 1918   IRT   ⑥

The original station at Grand Central was under 42nd Street near Vanderbilt Avenue, on the east-west line between Grand Central and Times Square. Under Contract 3, the present station was built under the east end of the new (1913) Grand Central Terminal, where a diagonal section of track shifts the east side extension from Park to Lexington Avenue.

The mosaic emblems are almost certainly the work of Jay Van Everen, whose bridge plaques at 125th Street are similar in design, especially the strong triangular background pieces. By choosing a head-on view of a 19th-century bell-stacked engine complete with cow catcher, he made a clear connection with the railroad terminal above.

In 1915 the Public Service Commission oversaw the replacement of the 1866 bridge which carried elevated lines over the Harlem River. A year later Jay Van Everen designed mosaic plaques for this station on the IRT's Lexington Avenue extension. It is likely that the new bridge, with its center-bearing drawspan, served as his model.

Van Everen's oil study—in the permanent collection of the Whitney Museum—is a careful rendering of such a bridge, showing the tender's house and a church steeple at the left. The execution in mosaic is remarkably faithful in design, though the palette is more somber: mostly browns and blues and white, eliminating the fanciful pinks and purples in Van Everen's study.

This is one of the most significant ceramic installations because the plaques are so large and so many remain in good condition and because there is documentation, in the oil study, of the artist's intentions.

The decorative work at Main Street has a distinctly different feeling from the ceramics in earlier Dual Contracts stations. It is far more sleek and stylized. In the frieze that runs along the wall above the name panel there are abstract suggestions of three structures. Most likely they represent (from left to right) three nearby historic buildings: St. George's Episcopal Church, whose congregation has been meeting on Main Street for almost 300 years; the hip-roofed Friends Meeting House on Northern Boulevard, the oldest house of worship in New York City; and the 17th-century John Bowne house, with its peaked roof and fat chimney, pictured in blue mosaic with an 'M' for Main Street. The tower and peaked roof, sometimes in the blue mosaic and sometimes in larger tile, are repeated in colorful wide bands around columns on the platform.

Many of the Dual Contracts stations built during the teens and early twenties had name panels and friezes of the sort shown here at 49th Street. Though most of the BMT stations along Broadway have been covered with large tiles and given colorful porcelain enamel name panels, examples of the mosaic work can still be found in many IRT stations of that period.

The original ceramic work at 49th Street disappeared in the early seventies when the station walls were resurfaced with the same bright orange tile that was used at Bowling Green. The work was done as part of a renovation—directed by the architect Philip Johnson—which also installed sound-absorbing materials and new lighting. Mr. Johnson was quoted in a 1970 *New York Times* article: "Cheer is the word, like a big shopping center."

The mosaic picture is a faithful reproduction of a Lossing-Barrett drawing in the *New York Common Council Manual* of 1865. The drawing is entitled "Junction of Broadway and the Bowery Road, 1828." (The date is actually included in the mosaic.) It shows the 'union' of the two roads, with tall trees and three chimneys above the distinctive rooflines of the house at the northwest edge of what was then the park—enlarged a few years later into the present Union Square.

The plaque is unusual in that the mark of the artist, Jay Van Everen, is actually included in the mosaic, to the right of the date. It is formed from his initials—JVE—joined to create a monogram: . This signature appears on two other original designs: the bridge for 125th Street on the Lexington line; and the 1909 Metropolitan Life tower, a plaque planned for the station at 23rd Street at Madison Square but not actually used. (Both of those oil studies are in the Whitney Museum's collection.) There is no evidence that Van Everen used this mark on any of his non-subway paintings.

This plaque is one of the best known, and, luckily, five of them near the token booth on the southbound side were preserved when the station walls were covered by modern tile. It is often referred to as "the lovers' bridge and Aaron Burr's house," but I.N.P. Stokes, writing about an 1812 painting in his *New York Past and Present: 1524-1939*, described it differently:

The "Arch," or Stone Bridge, was probably erected during the Revolution to facilitate access to the fortifications near the Collect Pond. By 1782 Broadway (or Great George Street, as it was then called) had been formally extended across and beyond the ditch, clearly indicating the existence of a bridge at this time. The large double house, on the s.w. corner of Broadway and Canal Street, is the "Stone Bridge Tavern" often referred to in writings of the period. The canal or ditch ran from the Collect to the North River at Canal Street and to the East River at Catherine Street. In early times it is supposed to have been navigable in canoes. It was formalized and a sewer constructed through the street in 1819.

Jay Van Everen designed the mosaic plaque. He was probably guided, as in his design for Union Square, by a Lossing-Barrett drawing—almost identical to the one Stokes described—in the *New York Common Council Manual* of 1865.

City Hall   January 5, 1918   BMT

The artist—probably Jay Van Everen—designed a faithful rendition of the old City Hall cupola, complete with a suggestion of the statue of Justice on top of the dome. The sky and clouds are rendered in angular chunks of blue and white tile, very similar to Van Everen's work in the 125th Street station on the Lexington Avenue line. All of the plaques remain visible: thirty-five along each tunnel wall.

This station was built under Broadway at the spot where Beach's experimental pneumatic subway had run nearly fifty years earlier. In fact, the tiny earlier tunnel was incorporated into the new one.

Whitehall   January 5, 1918   BMT

Originally known as Peter Stuyvesant's Great House, or townhouse (to distinguish it from his country house on Great Bouwerie at 14th Street and Second Avenue), this handsome white stone building became New York's Government House and acquired the name 'Whitehall'.

It is not clear which artist designed this plaque, but the view of the house as well as the placement of trees, ships and hills suggest that it was copied from one of Hollyer's *Old New York* views.

Although some thirty plaques remain visible on each side of the tunnel, many have suffered from water damage which has eroded the mortar holding the colorful tile borders.

Their strong, clean design makes these plaques especially effective, even from across the tracks. They show the sedate dome and portico of the old Kings County Courthouse surrounded by a border of large, cheerful tiles (almost identical to the borders at Whitehall).

A western entrance to the station is at the side of the Church of the Holy Trinity, whose name is announced in a mosaic panel at the foot of the subway stairs. At each end of the panel there is a mosaic Gothic window celebrating the fine stained glass which William Jay Bolton created for the church in the 1840's. His Holy Trinity windows were among the earliest in the United States and have been undergoing renovation.

Also at the entrance by the church, until recently, was one of the last "Subway" lampposts in the green and white colors of the BMT.

Wilson Avenue   July 14, 1928   BMT

There is a bold frieze consisting of horizontal 'crazy-quilt' panels of 2-5 inch primary-colored tiles, joined and surrounded by a finer mosaic border. (Similar treatment can be found in other stations on this line, for example at the adjacent Bushwick Avenue/Aberdeen Street station.) Occasionally the frieze is interrupted by a mosaic 'W' set in a hexagonal frame.

The ceramic work is found only on the inbound track of this station, unique in having an underground platform inbound and an elevated platform outbound.

Wilson Avenue is one of the last stations decorated with a mosaic frieze. The IND stations, built by the City, did not have such decoration.

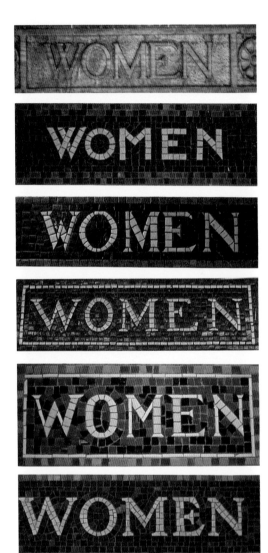